1001

"Twitter Quotes"

1001

"Twitter Quotes"

The Best Intelligent, Beautiful and Wise Quotes posted on Twitter

####

Compiled and Arranged by
Carlos and Sandra Caro

MOLECOOLAR

Molecoolar books are available at special discounts when purchased in bulk for premiums and sales promotions as well as for fund-raising or educational use. Special editions or book excerpts can also be created to specification. For details, contact the Special Editions Director at the address below or send an email to specialeditions@molecoolar.com

Molecoolar, LLC
5403 Old Lodge Dr
Houston, TX 77066-1620
Printed in the U.S.A.

First printing May 2011
ISBN: 978-0-9837279-2-7

Dedications

- To our dearest son Carl Jefferson.

- To our parents Carlos, Carlos, Norberta, and Socorro.

- To our brothers and sisters German, Ana Bertha, Walter Ansberto, Edgar, Ana Laura, and Carlos.

Acknowledgements

- All the genius people throughout history.

- All the people who want to become a better person every day.

- All the people who shared their #knowledge and #experience for a #better life.

- All the people who RTed these wonderful #quotes.

- All the people @Twitter for creating this incredible social network.

CONTENTS

Part 2
Remarkable Quotes

Introduction

Since the beginning of history, mankind has relayed their knowledge and experience through different ways: on painted stone, sculpted stone, wood, leather, pulp rags, papyrus, and paper. At the end of the 20th century, the internet was invented and with it, a new form of communication began to unfold.

Then at the beginning of the 21st century, a group of very smart people created Twitter, an incredible network of individuals and organizations interconnected through mobile and desktop devices where they share small phrases between them for all of us to see and learn from them. We are now living in a digital era where knowledge and experience are transmitted through electronic displays instantly to the whole world.

Some of these phrases shared on this network are quotes, statements or passages said by persons from different eras and places. We have gathered a collection of the best quotes posted on Twitter. They are full of intelligence, beauty and wisdom. The first five hundred and thirty six quotes range from success to goal quotes, from love to family quotes, from friendship to imagination quotes, from God to happiness quotes.

The rest of the book is filled with individually selected quotes for you to discover. Read them and fill yourself of the best advise and expertise you can find. Learn from them and put them in action or just think how they can add more meaning to your life, your love ones, and the people around you.

We gathered these quotes specially for you and we are happy that chose our book.

Wishing you a wonderful reading!

– CARLOS and SANDRA CARO

Part 1
Special Quotes

Chapter 1

Change Quotes

1 "One could change the World with one hundred & forty characters" – @Jack

2 "The key to change... is to let go of fear." – Rosanne Cash

3 "Resolve to be a master of change rather than a victim of change." – Brian Tracy

4 "We cannot change our memories, but we can change their meaning and the power they have over us." – David Seamans

5 "Change indeed is painful; yet ever needful; and if Memory have its force and worth, so also has Hope." – Thomas Carlyle

6 "Don't be too organized for your future. Life is unpredictable. Things change." – Wilson Kanadi

7 "Change the changeable, accept the unchangeable, and remove yourself from the unacceptable." – Denis Waitley

8 "No matter what people tell you, words and ideas can change the world." – Robin Williams

9 "You really can change the world if you care enough." – Marian Wright Edelman

10 "If things go wrong, you hit a dead end–as you will–it's just life's way of saying time to change course." – Oprah

11 "Books can be dangerous. The best ones should be labeled "This could change your life." – Helen Exley

12 "If you accept the expectations of others, especially negative ones, then you never will change the outcome." – Michael Jordan

13 "Intelligence is the ability to adapt to change." – Stephen Hawking

14 "Money & success don't change people; they merely amplify what is already there." – Will Smith

15 "Never doubt that a small group of thoughtful, committed citizens can change the world. It's the only thing that ever has." – Margaret Mead

16 "I never wanted to be a businessman, I just wanted to change the world." – Richard Branson

17 "Be the change you want to see in the world." – Mahatma Ghandi

18 "Not everything that is faced can be changed, but nothing can be changed until it is faced." – Lucille Ball

19 "Change your thoughts & you change your world." – Norman Vincent Peale

20 "A small group of thoughtful people could change the world. Indeed, it's the only thing that ever has." – Margaret Mead

21 "Change in all things is sweet." – Aristotle

22 "Forgiveness does not change the past, but it does enlarge the future." – Paul Boese

23 "We must become the change we want to see." – Mahatma Gandhi

24 "It's not your position in life; it's the disposition you have which will change your position." – Dr. David McKinley

25 "The past cannot be changed. The future is yet in your power." – Hugh White

Chapter 2

Success Quotes

26 "Success is walking from failure to failure with no loss of enthusiasm." – Winston Churchill

27 "Success is the maximum utilization of the ability that you have." – Zig Ziglar

28 "The only place where success comes before work is in the dictionary." – Vidal Sassoon

29 "Coming together is a beginning; keeping together is progress; working together is success." – Henry Ford

30 "Successful people are always looking for opportunities to help others. Unsuccessful people are asking, What's in it for me?" – Brian Tracy

31 "Try not to be a man of success, but rather try to become a man of value." – Albert Einstein

32 "There is only one success – to be able to spend your life in your own way." – Christopher Morley

33 "Without continual growth and progress, such words as improvement, achievement, and success have no meaning." – Benjamin Franklin

34 "Success does not consist in never making blunders, but in never making the same one a second time." – Josh Billings

35 "The secret of success in life is for a man to be ready for his opportunity when it comes." – Earl of Beaconsfield

36 "Success is liking yourself, liking what you do, and liking how you do it." – Maya Angelou

37 "The road to success and the road to failure are almost exactly the same." – Colin R. Davis

38 "It's not that successful people are givers; it is that givers are successful people." – Patti Thor

39 "Requirements for major success are: 1st being in the right place at the right time & 2nd, doing something about it." – Ray Kroc

40 "Success is not to be pursued, it is to be attracted by the person you become." – Jim Rohn

41 "Don't confuse fame with success. Madonna is one; Helen Keller is the other." – Erma Bombeck

42 "The talent of success is nothing more than doing what you can do, well." – Henry W. Longfellow

43 "A little more persistence, a little more effort, and what seemed hopeless failure may turn to glorious success." – Elbert Hubbard

44 "Success is not the key to happiness. Happiness is the key to success." – Albert Schweitzer

45 "Success is the sum of small efforts, repeated day in and day out." – Robert Collier

46 "Your chances of success in any undertaking can always be measured by your belief in yourself." – Robert Collier

47 "Success is simply a matter of luck. Ask any failure." – Earl Nightingale

48 "It's how you deal with failure that determines how you achieve success." – David Feherty

49 "I don't measure a man's success by how high he climbs, but how high he bounces when he hits bottom." – George Patton

50 "Honor your calling. Everybody has one. Trust your heart and success will come to you." – Oprah

51 "Success is peace of mind which is a direct result of knowing u did your best to become the best that u are capable of being." – John Wooden

52 "If you are afraid of failure you don't deserve to be successful!" – Charles Barkley

53 "You cannot climb the ladder of success dressed in the costume of failure." – Zig Ziglar

54 "Without self–discipline, success is impossible, period." – Lou Holtz

55 "I'd rather be a failure in something that I love than a success in something that I hate." – George Burns

56 "Four things for success: work & pray, think & believe." – Norman Peale

57 "You never achieve success unless you like what you are doing." – Dale Carnegie

58 "Success isn't measured by money or power or social rank. Success is measured by your discipline & inner peace." – Mike Ditka

59 "I don't know the key to success, but the key to failure is trying to please everybody." – Bill Cosby

60 "Not everyone can be successful in business because some people are afraid to take the risk and some depends on others." – Faree Imaan

61 "Success has many fathers, while failure is an orphan." – English proverbs

62 "The most important single ingredient in the formula of success is knowing how to get along with people." – Theodore Roosevelt

63 "Believe you will be successful and you will." – Dale Carnegie

64 "The making of friends who are real friends is the best token we have of a man's success in life." – Edward Hale

65 "I couldn't wait for success, so I went ahead without it." – Jonathan Winters

66 "The key to successful leadership today is influence, not authority." – Kenneth Blanchard

Chapter 3

Love Quotes

67 "It is not thinking, nor even time that heals... it is love." – Anonymous

68 "Love is a friendship set to music." – E. Joseph Cossman

69 "Love is the master key which opens the gates of happiness." – Oliver Wendell Holmes

70 "We have not the love of greatness, but the love of the love of greatness." – Thomas Carlyle

71 "Better to have loved a short man than never to have loved a tall." – G. K. Chesterton

72 "Mother love is the fuel that enables a normal human being to do the impossible." – Marion C. Garretty

73 "Every time you smile at someone, it is an action of love, a gift to that person, a beautiful thing." – Mother Teresa

74 "Hate cannot drive out hate; only love can do that." – Rev. Martin Luther King, Jr

75 "Love is the only force capable of transforming an enemy to a friend." – Martin Luther King Jr.

76 "The best portion of a good man's life is in his little nameless, unremembered acts of kindness & of love." – W. Wordsworth

77 "To serve. You only need a heart full of grace and a soul generated by love." – Martin Luther King

78 "Judge nothing, you will be happy. Forgive everything, you will be happier. Love everything, you will be happiest." – Sri Chinmoy

79 "All you need is love. But a little chocolate now & then doesn't hurt." – Charles M. Schulz

80 "Love is the joy of the good, the wonder of the wise, the amazement of the Gods." – Plato

81 "Love is the force that ignites the spirit & binds teams together." – Phil Jackson

82 "In this life we cannot always do great things. But we can do small things with great love." – Mother Teresa

83 "Your task is not to seek for love, but merely to seek & find all the barriers within yourself that you have built against it." – Rumi

84 "Once you have learned to love, You will have learned to live." – Unknown

85 "When we cannot get what we love, we must love what is within our reach." – French Proverb

86 "Where there is love, there is life." – Mahatma Gandhi

87 "Never let a problem to be solved become more important than a person to be loved." – Barbra Johnson

88 "If we really want to love we must learn how to forgive." – Mother Teresa

89 "It's easy to halve the potato where there's love." – Irish Proverb

90 "A man is not where he lives, but where he loves." – Latin Proverb

91 "Who travels for love finds a thousand miles not longer than one." – Japanese Proverb

92 "A heart in love with beauty never grows old." – Turkish Proverb

93 "A heart that loves is always young." – Greek Proverb

94 "He who is not impatient is not in love." – Italian Proverb

95 "Love is composed of a single soul inhabiting two bodies." – Aristotle

96 "To understand your parents' love you must raise children yourself." – Chinese Proverbs

97 "Love is like dew that falls on both nettles & lilies." – Swedish Proverb

98 "Does thou love life? Then do not squander time, for that's the stuff life is made of." – Benjamin Franklin

99 "If you are lucky enough to find a way of life you love, you have to find the courage to live it." – John Irving

100 "In love with life I live the subtlest of passions, live like a gypsy, each day a different house, each night under the stars." – Rumi

101 "Darkness cannot drive out darkness; only light can do that. Hate cannot drive out hate; only love can do that." – Martin Luther King, Jr.

102 "If you love somebody, let them go, for if they return, they were always yours. And if they don't, they never were." – Khalil Gibran

103 "The day you catch an idea you fall in love with, even a small one, is a beautiful day." – David Lynch

Chapter 4

Do Quotes

104 "Do or do not, there is no try." – Yoda

105 "Tell everyone what you want to do and someone will want to help you do it." – W. Clement Stone

106 "If you cannot do great things, do small things in a great way." – Napoleon Hill

107 "If you always do what you've always done, you'll always get what you've always got!" – Alan Scott

108 "Yes, you can be a dreamer and a doer too, if you will remove one word from your vocabulary: impossible." – Robert Schuller

109 "Never leave that 'til tomorrow which you can do today." –Benjamin Franklin

110 "Do not look for approval except for the consciousness of doing your best." – Andrew Carnegie

Chapter 5

Leadership Quotes

111 "Innovation distinguishes between a leader and a follower." – Steve Jobs

112 "A leader is one who knows the way, goes the way, and shows the way." – John Maxwell

113 "No man will make a great leader who wants to do it all himself, or to get all the credit for doing it." – Andrew Carnegie

114 "Speech inspires. Action produces. Outstanding leaders blend speech with action." – Reed Markham

115 "There are 4 kinds of leaders: those you laugh at,those you hate,those you love & those who you don't even know are leaders." – Bill Bradley

116 "The real leader has no need to lead—he is content to point the way." – Henry Miller

117 "Management is doing things right; leadership is doing the right things." – Peter Drucker"

118 "Without initiative, leaders are simply workers in leadership positions." – Bo Bennett

119 "Do not wait for leaders; do it alone, person to person." – Mother Teresa

120 "The function of leadership is to produce more leaders, not more followers." – Ralph Nader

121 "A leader has the vision and conviction that a dream can be achieved. He inspires the power and energy to get it done." – Ralph Lauren

122 "Leadership is not domination, but the art of persuading people to work towards a common goal." – Daniel Goleman

Chapter 6

Goal Quotes

123 "If what you are doing is not moving you towards your goals, then it's moving you away from your goals." – Brian Tracy

124 "Obstacles are things a person sees when he takes his eyes off his goal." – E. Joseph Cossman

125 "A goal is a dream with a deadline." – Napoleon Hill

126 "If you want to reach a goal, you must 'see the reaching' in your own mind before you actually arrive at your goal." – Zig Ziglar

127 "Without goals and plans to reach them, you are like a ship that has set sail with no destination." – F. Dodson

128 "You are never too old to set another goal or to dream a new dream."– C.S. Lewis

129 "To achieve happiness, we should make certain that we are never without an important goal."– Ralph Waldo Emerson

130 "When it is obvious that the goals cannot be reached, don't adjust the goals, adjust the action steps." – Confucious

131 "The big secret in life is that there is no big secret. Whatever your goal, you can get there if you're willing to work."– Oprah Winfrey

132 "If your life goal is to get by you're barely alive." – RBs Keys

133 "The most important thing about goals is having one." – Geoffrey Abert

134 "Goals are the fuel in the furnace of achievement." – Brian Tracy

135 "Nothing can stop the man with the right mental attitude from achieving his goal." – Thomas Jefferson

136 "People with goals succeed because they know where they're going. It's that simple." – Earl Nightingale

137 "You need to overcome the tug of people against you as you reach for high goals." – George Patton

138 "Set peace of mind as your highest goal, and organize your life around it." – Brian Tracy

139 "Happiness is not a goal; it is a by–product." – Eleanor Roosevelt

140 "Any person who selects a goal in life which can be fully achieved, has already defined his own limitations." – Cavett Robert

141 "Until you commit your goals to paper, you have intentions that are seeds without soil." — Anonymous

142 "The road leading to a goal does not separate you from the destination; it is essentially a part of it." – Charles DeLint

Chapter 7

Family Quotes

143 "Man is the head of the family, woman the neck that turns the head." – Chinese Proverb

144 "Govern a family as you would cook a small fish, very gently." – Chinese Proverbs

Chapter 8

Friendship Quotes

145 "Don't make friends who are comfortable to be with. Make friends who will force you to lever yourself up." – Thomas J. Watson

146 "The only way to have a friend is to be one." – Ralph Waldo Emerson

147 "As a child my number one best friend was the librarian in my grade school. I actually believed all those books belonged to her." – Erma Bombeck

148 "A friendly look, a kindly smile, one good act, & life's worthwhile." – Unknown

149 "Be slow to fall into friendship; but when thou art in, continue firm & constant." – Socrates

150 "A true friend is one who thinks you are a good egg even if you are half–cracked." – Author Unknown

151 "Be slow in choosing a friend, but slower in changing him." – Scottish Proverb

152 "Awards become corroded, friends gather no dust." – Jesse Owens

153 "You know you've read a good book when you turn the last page & feel a little as if you have lost a friend." – Paul Sweeney

154 "The road to a friend's house is never long." – Danish Proverb

155 "A friend is someone who is there for you when he'd rather be anywhere else." – Len Wein

156 "A mere friend will agree with you, but a real friend will argue." – Russian Proverb

157 "My friend is he who will tell me my faults in private." – Solomon Ibn Gabirol

158 "Only your real friends will tell you when your face is dirty." – Sicilian Proverb

159 "Do not use a hatchet to remove a fly from your friend's forehead." – Chinese Proverb

160 "With true friends, even water drunk together is sweet enough."– Chinese Proverb

161 "Friendship with oneself is all important because without it one cannot be friends with anybody else in the world." – Eleanor Roosevelt

162 "In poverty & other misfortunes of life, true friends are a sure refuge." – Aristotle

163 "The best friend is the man who in wishing me well wishes it for my sake." – Aristotle

164 "For the friendship of two, the patience of one is required." – Indian Proverb

165 "There are plenty of acquaintances in the world; but very few real friends." – Chinese Proverbs

166 "Hold a true friend with both your hands." – Nigerian Proverb

167 "A friend you have to buy; enemies you get for nothing." – Jewish Proverb

168 "Who ceases to be a friend never was one." – Greek Proverb

169 "A man should choose a friend who is better than himself." – Chinese Proverbs

170 "No person is your friend who demands your silence, or denies your right to grow." – Alice Walker

Chapter 9

Action Quotes

171 "Action speaks louder than words but not nearly as often." – Mark Twain

172 "An ounce of action is worth a ton of theory." – Ralph Waldo Emerson

173 "The more you are willing to accept responsibility for your actions, the more credibility you will have." – Brian Koslow

174 "Vision without action is daydreaming and action without vision is a nightmare." – Anon

175 "The superior man is modest in his speech, but exceeds in his actions." – Confucius

176 "Doubt, of whatever kind, can be ended by action alone." – Thomas Carlyle

177 "Everything you want is out there waiting for you to ask. Everything you want also wants you. Take action to get it." – Jack Canfield

178 "When we can recognize&forgive ignorant actions of the past, we gain the strength 2 constructively solve the problems of the present." – Dalai Lama

179 "Repetition is the mother of learning, the father of action, which makes it the architect of accomplishment." – Zig Ziglar

180 "Create a definite plan for carrying out your desire, and begin at once, whether you're ready or not, to put it into action." – Napoleon Hill

Chapter 10

Work Quotes

181 "Choose a job you love, and you will never have to work a day in your life." –Confucius

182 "I've always worked very, very hard, and the harder I worked, the luckier I got." – Alan Bond

183 "I have not failed. I've just found 10,000 ways that won't work." – Thomas Edison

184 "Far and away the best prize that life has to offer is the chance to work hard at work worth doing." – Theodore Roosevelt

185 "The beginning is the most important part of any work." – Plato

186 "Plans are only good intentions unless they immediately degenerate into hard work." – Peter Drucker.

187 "We either make ourselves miserable, or we make ourselves happy. The amount of work is the same." – Carlos Castaneda

188 "If u really want something, & really work hard, & take advantage of opportunities, & never give up, u will find a way." – Jane Goodall

189 "When your work speaks for itself, don't interrupt." – Henry J. Kaiser

190 "I've got a theory that if you give 100% all of the time, somehow things will work out in the end." – Larry Bird

191 "Win or lose you will never regret working hard, making sacrifices, being disciplined or focusing too much." – John Smith

192 "The Six W's: Work will win when wishing won't." – Todd Blackledge

193 "The more I want to get something done, the less I call it work." – Richard Bach

194 "Work expands so as to fill the time available." – English proverbs

195 "Pleasure in the job puts perfection in the work." – Aristotle

196 "If you want to leave your footprints on the sands of time, be sure you're wearing work shoes." – Author Unknown

197 "When you're following your energy and doing what you want all the time, the distinction between work and play dissolves." – Shakti Gawain

198 "If the power to do hard work is not a skill, it's the best possible substitute for it." – James Garfield

199 "The secret of joy in work is contained in one word – excellence. To know how to do something well is to enjoy it." – Pearl Buck

200 "Common sense is genius dressed up in work clothes." – Ralph Waldo Emerson

201 "Make the workmanship surpass the materials." – Ovid

Chapter 11

Imagination Quotes

202 "Imagination is more important than knowledge." –Albert Einstein

203 "Imagination is the highest kite one can fly." – Lauren Bacall

204 "Logic will get you from A to B. Imagination will take you everywhere." – Albert Einstein

205 "Live out of your imagination instead of out of your memory." – Fortune Cookie

206 "When one paints an ideal, one does not need to limit one's imagination."– Ellen Key

207 "Imagination is everything. It is the preview of life's coming attractions." – Albert Einstein

208 "There is a vision for my life that is greater then my imagination can hold." – Oprah

209 "Limitations live only in our minds. But if we use our imaginations, our possibilities become limitless." – Jamie Paolinetti

210 "The world is but a canvas to the imagination." – Henry David Thoreau

211 "Imagination is the true magic carpet." – Norman Peale

212 "Imagination will often carry us to worlds that never were. But without it we go nowhere." – Carl Sagan

213 "There are no such things as limits to growth, as there are no limits on the human capacity for intelligence, imagination, and wonder." – Reagan

Chapter 12

God Quotes

214 "God's delays are not God's denials." – Robert Schuller

215 "God sometimes removes a person from your life for your protection. Don't run after them." – Rick Warren

216 "God can dream a bigger dream for you then you could ever dream for yourself." – Oprah

217 "God doesn't require us to succeed; he only requires that you try." – Mother Teresa

218 "Every evening I turn my worries over to God. He's going to be up all night anyway." – Mary C. Crowley

219 "In nature we see where God has been. In our fellow man, we see where He is still at work." – Robert Brault

220 "What God intended for you goes far beyond anything you can imagine." – Oprah

221 "Our prayers should be for blessings in general, for God knows best what is good for us." – Socrates

222 "What do you think of God, the teacher asked. After a pause, the young pupil replied, "He's not a think, he's a feel." – Paul Frost

223 "I can't believe that God put us on this earth to be ordinary." – Lou Holtz

224 "I would rather die than do something, which I know to be a sin, or to be against God's will." – Joan of Arc

225 "You are a child of God. Your playing small does not serve the world. There is nothing enlightened about shrinking." – Marianne Williamson

226 "God gave burdens, also shoulders." – Yiddish proverb

227 "God's gifts put man's best dreams to shame." – Elizabeth Browning

228 "Talent is God given. Be humble. Fame is man–given. Be grateful. Conceit is self–given. Be careful." – John Wooden

Chapter 13

The Lord Quotes

229 "I'm working for the Lord, and even though the Lord's pay isn't very high, his retirement program is." – George Foreman

Chapter 14

Attitude Quotes

230 "Attitude is a little thing that makes a big difference." – Winston Churchill

231 "Your attitude can take you forward or your attitude can take you down. The choice is always yours!" – Catherine Pulsifer

232 "Our attitude towards others determines their attitude towards us." – Earl Nightingale

233 "The only disability in life is a bad attitude."
– Scott Hamilton

234 "Our environment, the world in which we live and work, is a mirror of our attitudes and expectations." – Earl Nightingale

235 "Procrastination is attitude's natural assassin. There is nothing so fatiguing as an uncompleted task." – William James

Chapter 15

Happiness Quotes

236 "Money won't make you happy… but everybody wants to find out for themselves." – Zig Ziglar

237 "In about the same degree as you are helpful, you will be happy." –Karl Reiland

238 "A happy person is not a person in a certain set of circumstances, but rather a person with a certain set of attitudes." – Hugh Downs

239 "If you really want to be happy, always try to do what's right." – Bill Blackman

240 "Be happy in the moment, that's enough. Each moment is all we need, not more." – Mother Teresa

241 "To be happy, you have to give something back." – Oprah

242 "It's never too late – never too late to start over, never too late to be happy." – Jane Fonda

243 "Trust yourself. Create the kind of self that you will be happy to live with all your life." – Golda Meir

244 "Being miserable is a habit. Being happy is a habit. The choice is yours." – Tom Hopkins

245 "Very little is needed to make a happy life; it is all within yourself, in your way of thinking." – Marcus Aurelius

246 "My advice to you is get married: if you find a good wife you'll be happy; if not, you'll become a philosopher." – Socrates

247 "Happiness often sneaks in through a door you didn't know you left open." – John Barrymore

248 "The first recipe of happiness – avoid too lengthy meditations on the past." – Andre Maurois

249 "That is happiness – to be dissolved into something complete and great." – Willa Cather

250 "Happiness is not something you postpone for the future; it is something you design for the present." – Jim Rohn

251 "In the pursuit of happiness, the difficulty lies in knowing when you have caught up." – R.H. Grenville

252 "Happiness gives us the energy which is the basis of health." – Henri–Frédéric Amiel

253 "Happiness is found in doing, not merely possessing." – Napoleon Hill

254 "The person born with a talent they are meant to use will find their greatest happiness in using it." – Johann Wolfgang Von Goethe

255 "Happiness is like a kiss. You must share it to enjoy it. –Bernard Meltzer

256 "I want to say without hesitation that the purpose of our life is happiness." – 14th Dalai Lama

257 "The medals don't mean anything and the glory doesn't last. It's all about your happiness." – Jackie Joyner–Kersee

258 "Remember happiness doesn't depend upon who you are or what you have; it depends solely on what you think." – Dale Carnegie

259 "Happiness cannot come from without. It must come from within." – Helen Keller

260 "For every minute you are angry you lose sixty seconds of happiness." – Ralph Waldo Emerson

261 "Happiness is when what you think, what you say, and what you do are in harmony." – Gandhi

262 "Happiness depends upon ourselves." – Aristotle

263 "Happiness does not depend on your circumstances; it depends on your will. It's a choice that you make." – Joel Osteen

Chapter 16

Enthusiasm Quotes

264 "In the realm of ideas everything depends on enthusiasm. In the real world all rests on perseverance." – Johann Wolfgang von Goethe

265 "Enthusiasm can turn pessimists into optimists, losers into winners, and average people into champions." – Reed B Markham

266 "Nothing great was ever achieved without enthusiasm." – Ralph Waldo Emerson

267 "You can do anything if you have enthusiasm. Enthusiasm is the yeast that makes your hopes rise to the stars." – Henry Ford

268 "A person can succeed at almost anything for which they have unlimited enthusiasm." – Charles M. Schwab

269 "If you aren't fired with enthusiasm, you will be fired with enthusiasm." – Vince Lombardi

270 "Act enthusiastic and you will be enthusiastic." – Dale Carnegie

271 "Be interesting, be enthusiastic... & don't talk too much." – Norman Peale

Chapter 17

Learn Quotes

272 "Learn to say 'no' to the good so you can say 'yes' to the best." – John Maxwell

273 "Your most unhappy customers are your greatest source of learning." – Bill Gates

274 "The most valuable thing you can make is a mistake – you can't learn anything from being perfect." – Adam Osborne

275 "Learn to say 'no' to the good so you can say 'yes' to the best." – John Maxwell

276 "We grow because we struggle, we learn and overcome." – R C Allen

277 "View life as a continuous learning experience." – Denis Waitley

278 "We could never learn to be brave & patient, if there were only joys in the world." – Helen Keller

279 "Finish each day & be done with it. You have done what you could. Learn from it. tomorrow is a new day." – Ralph Waldo Emerson

280 "I have learned over th years that when 1's mind is made up, this diminishes fear; knowing what must be done does away with fear." – Rosa Parks

281 "The trick is to learn to check your ego at the door and start checking your gut instead." – Oprah

282 "I learned that courage was not the absence of fear, but the triumph over it." – Nelson Mandela

283 "Do not confine your children to your own learning, for they were born in another time." – Chinese Proverbs

284 "Learning is a treasure that will follow its owner everywhere." – Chinese Proverbs

285 "Those who do not learn from history are doomed to repeat it." – English proverbs

286 "I learn something new about the game almost every time I step on the course." – Ben Hogan

287 "We learn as much from sorrow as from joy, as much from illness as from health – and indeed perhaps more." – Pearl Buck

Chapter 18

Effort Quotes

288 "Effort only fully releases its reward after a person refuses to quit." – Napoleon Hill

289 "Satisfaction does not come with achievement, but with effort. Full effort is full victory." – Mahatma Gandhi

290 "It is always the start that requires the greatest effort." – James Cash Penney

Chapter 19

Dream Quotes

291 "Too many of us are not living our dreams because we are living our fears." – Les Brown

292 "You cannot dream yourself into a character; you must hammer and forge yourself one." – Henry David Thoreau

293 "The only place where your dream becomes impossible is in your own thinking." – Robert H. Schuller

294 "Explore. Dream. Discover." – Mark Twain

295 "I have spread my dreams beneath your feet. Tread softly because you tread on my dreams." – W.B. Yeats

296 "A dream is a compelling vision you see in your heart thats too big to accomplish without others help." – Chris Hodges

297 "You can't put a limit on anything. The more you dream, the farther you get." – Michael Phelps

298 "The biggest adventure you can take is to live the life of your dreams." – Oprah

299 "Whatever you can do, or dream you can, begin it. Boldness has genius, power, magic in it." – Goethe

300 "An athlete cannot run with money in his pockets. He must run with hope in his heart & dreams in his head." – Emil Zatopek

301 "When you follow the dream in your heart, you're energised, inspired, & motivated." – Dr. John F. Demartini

302 "You see things & you say, why? But I dream things that never were & I say, why not?" – George Bernard Shaw

303 "The future belongs to those who believe in the beauty of their dreams." – Eleanor Roosevelt

304 "Winners, imagine their dreams 1st. They want it with all their heart & expect it to come true. There's no other way to live." – Joe Montana

305 "Go after your dream, no matter how unattainable others think it is." – Linda Mastandrea

306 "I'd say it's been my biggest problem all my life.. it's money. It takes a lot of money to make these dreams come true." – Walt Disney

307 "The longer the night lasts, the more our dreams will be." – Chinese Proverbs

308 "Hope is the dream of a waking man." – Aristotle

309 "Dream different dreams while on the same bed." – Chinese Proverb

Chapter 20

Think Quotes

310 "As long as you're going to be thinking anyway, think big." – Donald Trump

311 "Positive thinking will let you do everything better than negative thinking will." – Zig Ziglar

312 "They can because they think they can." – Virgil

313 "A man who does not think for himself does not think at all." – Oscar Wilde

314 "I never think of the future – it comes soon enough." – Albert Einstein

315 "It's not what you are that holds you back, it's what you think you are not." – Denis Waitley

316 "Sooner or later, those who win are those who think they can." – Richard Bach

317 "Do the one thing you think you cannot do. Fail at it. Try again. Do better the second time." – Oprah

318 "Think like a queen. A queen is not afraid to fail. Failure is another steppingstone to greatness." – Oprah

319 "Whether or not you think you can or you cant. Either way, you are right!" – Henry Ford

320 "You must do the thing which you think you cannot do." – Eleanor Roosevelt

321 "Thinking: the talking of the soul with itself." – Plato

322 "The great creators–the thinkers, the artists, the scientists, the inventors–stood alone against the men of their time." – Ayn Rand

323 "If everyone is thinking alike, then somebody isn't thinking." – George S. Patton

324 "You can't have a better tomorrow if you're thinking about yesterday." – Charles Kettering

325 "I don't think anything is unrealistic if you believe you can do it." – Mike Ditka

326 "When you think positive, excellent thoughts you will be propelled toward greatness." – Joel Osteen

Chapter 21

Communication Quotes

327 "The most important thing in communication is to hear what isn't being said." – Peter F. Drucker

328 "Effective communication is 20% what you know and 80% how you feel about what you know." – Jim Rohn

Chapter 22

Accomplishment Quotes

329 "Accomplish something every day of your life." – Walter Annenberg

330 "He that is over–cautious will accomplish little." – Friedrich von Schiller

331 "Nothing builds self–esteem and self–confidence like accomplishment." – Thomas Carlyle

332 "The height of your accomplishments will equal the depth of your convictions." – William F. Scholavino

333 "To be yourself in a world that is constantly trying to make you something else is the greatest accomplishment." – Ralph Waldo Emerson

334 "No matter what accomplishments you make, somebody helped you." – Althea Gibson

335 "I always turn to the sports pages first, which records people's accomplishments. The front page has nothing but man's failures." – Earl Warren

336 "People of accomplishment rarely sat back & let things happen to them. They went out & happened to things." – Leonardo Da Vinci

Chapter 23

Future Quotes

337 "Let your hopes, not your hurts, shape your future." – Robert Schuller

338 "The best way to predict the future is to create it." – Peter Drucker

339 "Go for it now. The future is promised to no one." – Wayne Dyer

340 "The distinction between the past, present and future is only a stubbornly persistent illusion." – Albert Einstein

341 "When we have nothing to worry about we are not doing much, & not doing much may supply us with plenty of future worries." – Chinese Proverb

342 "The future starts today, not tomorrow." – Pope John Paul II

343 "The greatest danger to our future is apathy." – Jane Goodall

Chapter 24

Courage Quotes

344 "We cannot discover new oceans unless we have the courage to lose sight of the shore." – Anonymous

345 "All of us have moments in our lives that test our courage. Taking children into a house w/white carpet is one of them." – Erma Bombec

346 "Laughter rises out of tragedy, when you need it the most, and rewards you for your courage." – Erma Bombeck

347 "Do not lose courage in considering your own imperfections." – Saint Francis de Sales

348 "One man with courage is a majority." – Andrew Jackson

349 "Ingenuity plus courage plus work equals miracles." – Bob Richards

350 "You gain strength, courage, and confidence by every experience in which you really stop to look fear in the face." – Eleanor Roosevelt

351 "To me, there is no greater act of courage than being the one who kisses first." – Janeane Garofalo

352 "Courage is the art of being the only one who knows you're scared to death." – Earl Wilson

353 "Courage is knowing what not to fear." – Plato

354 "You will never do anything in this world without courage. It is the greatest quality of the mind next to honor." – Aristotle

355 "You can never cross the ocean unless you have the courage to lose sight of the shore." – Christopher Columbus

356 "Courage is like a muscle. We strengthen it with use." – Ruth Gordon

357 "Courage is grace under pressure." – Ernest Hemingway

358 "A man can get discouraged many times, but he is not a failure until he begins to blame somebody else and stops trying." – John Burroughs

359 "Courage is swimming with a great white shark without a cage" – Chip Esajian

Chapter 25

Kindness Quotes

360 "Kindness is a language which the deaf can hear and the blind can see." – Mark Twain

361 "As the sun makes ice melt, kindness causes misunderstanding, mistrust & hostility to evaporate." – Albert Schweitzer

362 "Remember there's no such thing as a small act of kindness. Every act creates a ripple with no logical end." – Adams

363 "No act of kindness, no matter how small, is ever wasted." – Aesop

364 "For attractive lips, speak words of kindness. For lovely eyes, seek out the good in people." – Audrey Hepburn

365 "Forget injuries, never forget kindnesses." – Confucius

366 "Kindness is more important than wisdom, and the recognition of this is the beginning of wisdom." – Theodore Isaac Rubin

Chapter 26

Reputation Quotes

367 "You can't build a reputation on what you're going to do." – Henry Ford

368 "The reputation of a thousand years may be determined by the conduct of one hour." – Japanese proverb

369 "It takes 20 years to build a reputation and five minutes to ruin it." – Warren Buffett

Chapter 27

Ideas Quotes

370 "Many great ideas go unexecuted, and many great executioners are without ideas. One without the other is worthless." – Tim Blixseth

371 "Pure mathematics is, in its way, the poetry of logical ideas." – Albert Einstein

372 "Better to have enough ideas for some of them to be wrong, than to be always right by having no ideas at all." – de Bono

373 "Million dollar ideas are a dime a dozen. The determination to see the idea through is what's priceless." – Robert Dieffenbach

374 "Great minds discuss ideas; average minds discuss events; small minds discuss people." – Eleanor Roosevelt

375 "Be strong in body, clean in mind, lofty in ideas." – James Naismith

376 "It is not once nor twice but times without number that the same ideas make their appearance in the world." – Aristotle

377 "All achievements, all earned riches, have their beginning in an idea." – Napoleon Hill

378 "Great ideas originate in the muscles." – Thomas A. Edison

Chapter 28

Knowledge Quotes

379 "A little knowledge is a dangerous thing." – English proverbs

380 "True knowledge exists in knowing that you know nothing." – Socrates

381 "All men by nature desire knowledge." – Aristotle

382 "Knowledge is the food of the soul." – Plato

383 "The only real security that a man will have in this world is a reserve of knowledge, experience and ability." – Henry Ford

384 "To be conscious that you are ignorant of the facts is a great step to knowledge." – Benjamin Disraeli

385 "Faith is a knowledge within the heart, beyond the reach of proof." – Khalil Gibran

Chapter 29

Life Quotes

386 "Life has no limitations, except the ones you make." –Les Brown

387 "The state of your life is nothing more than a reflection of your state of mind." – Wayne Dyer

388 "Our business in life is not to get ahead of others, but to get ahead of ourselves." – E. Joseph Cossman

389 "Life's problems wouldn't be called "hurdles" if there wasn't a way to get over them." – Unknown

390 "Life asks us to make measurable progress in reasonable time. That's why they make those fourth–grade chairs so small." – Jim Rohn

391 "Live a life as a monument to your soul." – Ayn Rand

392 "Our prime purpose in this life is to help others. And if you can't help them, at least don't hurt them." – Dalai Lama

393 "A moment's insight is sometimes worth a life's experience." – Oliver Wendell Holmes, Sr.

394 "You never know what life has in store for you, but I believe there are certain things one is meant to go through." – Gloria Estefan

395 "The length of our life is less important than its depth." – Mary David Fisher

396 "Life is the sum of all your choices." – Albert Camus

397 "If honor be your clothing, the suit will last a lifetime; but if clothing be your honor, it will soon be worn threadbare." –William Arnot

398 "I may not lead the most dramatic life, but in my brain it's War and Peace everyday." – Rufus Wainwright

399 "A life coach does for the rest of your life what a personal trainer does for your health and fitness." – Elaine MacDonald

400 "All life is an experiment. The more experiments you make the better." – Ralph Waldo Emerson

401 "The most rewarding things you do in life are often the ones that look like they cannot be done." – Arnold Palmer

402 "I've failed over & over & over again in my life & that is why I succeed." – Michael Jordan

403 "The only way to have a life is to commit to it like crazy." – Angelina Jolie

404 "The best thing to hold onto in life is each other." – Audrey Hepburn

405 "Giving is not just about being able to write a check. It's being able to touch somebody's life." – Oprah

406 "When planning for a year, plant corn. When planning for a decade, plant trees. When planning for life, educate people." – Chinese Proverbs

407 "I do the very best I can to look upon life with optimism and hope and looking forward to a better day." – Rosa Parks

408 "I could not, at any age, be content to take my place by the fireside and simply look on. Life was meant to be lived." – Eleanor Roosevelt

409 "A life is not important except in the impact it has on other lives." – Jackie Robinson

410 "As you walk down the fairway of life you must smell the roses, for you only get to play one round." – Ben Hogan

411 "Curiosity must be kept alive. One must never, for whatever reason, turn his back on life." – Eleanor Roosevelt

412 "You take your life in your own hands, and what happens? A terrible thing: no one to blame." – Erica Jong

413 "Your time is limited, so don't waste it living someone else's life." – Steve Jobs

414 "In life, as in sports, you'll try, & you'll sometimes fail. There'll be no apparent reward except to know that u did ur best." – Charles Lawrie

415 "Not life, but good life, is to be chiefly valued." – Socrates

416 "I don't want to get 2 the end of my life & find I lived just the length of it. I want 2 have lived the width of it as well." – Diane Ackerman

417 "Life is really simple, but we insist on making it complicated." – Confucius

418 "In life you are either a passenger or a pilot, it's your choice." – Unknown

419 "True wisdom comes to each of us when we realize how little we understand about life, ourselves, & the world around us." – Socrates

420 "One of the secrets of life is that all that is really worth the doing is what we do for others." – Levi Strauss

421 "You can't base your life on other people's expectations." – Stevie Wonder

422 "Life isn't about finding yourself, it's about creating yourself." – Unknown

423 "The essential thing in life is not conquering but fighting well." – Pierre de Coubertin

424 "Football is an honest game. It's true to life. It's a game about sharing. Football is a team game. So is life." – Joe Namath

425 "Life is either a daring adventure or nothing at all." – Helen Keller

426 "The best & most beautiful things in life cannot be seen, not touched, but are felt in the heart." – Helen Keller

427 "If daily you feel a sense of gratitude for the blessings of this life it will be a cushion & buffer when challenges arise." – Rose W–T

428 "You owe it to yourself to be the best you can possible be – in baseball and in life." – Pete Rose

429 "The resistance that you fight in the gym & the resistance that you fight in life can only build a strong character." – Arnold Schwarzenegger

430 "Once bitten by a snake, he/she is scared all his/her life at the mere sight of a rope." – Chinese Proverb

431 "The unexamined life is not worth living." – Socrates

432 "Thou wilt find rest from vain fancies if thou doest every act in life as though it were thy last." – Aristotle

433 "A man who views the world the same at fifty as he did at twenty has wasted thirty years of his life." – Muhammad Ali

434 "A smile will gain you ten more years of life."
– Chinese Proverb

435 "The measure of your life will not be in what
you accumulate, but in what you give away." – Wayne
Dyer

436 "The choices I make today will determine
the rest of my life!" – Ginny Dye

437 "A man who dares to waste one hour of time
has not discovered the value of life." – Charles
Darwin

438 "We make a living by what we get, we make
a life by what we give." – Sir Winston Churchill

439 "You will never be the person you can be if
pressure, tension and discipline are taken out of your
life." – James G. Bilkey

440 "When we remember we are all mad, the
mysteries disappear and life stands explained." –
Mark Twain

441 "We have committed the Golden Rule to memory; let us now commit it to life." – Edwin Markham

442 "Life is 10 percent what you make it, and 90 percent how you take it." – Irving Berlin

443 "Security is mostly a superstition. Life is either a daring adventure, or nothing." – Helen Keller

444 "Believe that life is worth living and your belief will help create the fact." – William James

445 "To some degree, you control your life by controlling your time." – Conrad Hilton

Chapter 30

Time Quotes

446 "One doesn't discover new lands without consenting to lose sight of the shore for a very long time." – Andre Gide

447 "Time Is What Prevents Everything From Happening At Once." – John Wheeler

448 "Time flies; but remember you are the navigator." – Author Unknown

449 "People never forget that helping hand especially when times are tough." – Catherine Pulsifer

450 "Failure is only the opportunity to begin again, this time more wisely." – Anonymous

451 "Most misfortunes are the result of misused time." – Napoleon Hill

452 "He takes men out of time and makes them feel eternity." – Ralph Waldo Emerson

453 "When someone shows you who they are, believe them the first time." – Oprah

454 "The greatest glory in living lies not in never falling, but in rising every time we fall." – Nelson Mandela

455 "Time you enjoy wasting, was not wasted." – John Lennon

456 "The time is always right to do what is right." – Martin Luther King Jr.

457 "In the right light, at the right time, everything is extraordinary." – Aaron Rose

458 "Look at everything as though you were seeing it either for the first or last time." – Betty Smith

459 "Employ your time in improving yourself by other men's writings, so that you shall gain easily what others have labored hard for." – Socrates

460 "An inch of time cannot be bought with an inch of gold." – Chinese Proverbs

461 "In times like these, it helps to recall that there have always been times like these." – Paul Harvey

462 "The bad news is time flies. The good news is you're the pilot." – Michael Altshuler

463 "In times of Universal deceit, telling the Truth becomes a revolutionary act." – George Orwell

464 "It does not matter how many times you get knocked down, but how many times you get up." – Vince Lombardi

Chapter 31

Sometimes Quotes

465 "Rough diamonds may sometimes be mistaken for worthless pebbles." – Sir Thomas Browne

466 "To deal with individual human needs at the everyday level can be noble sometimes." – Jimmy Carter

467 "Instead of trying to fit in, fight to stand out; sometimes you only get one look, one kiss, one moment!" – B.Aki

468 "Sometimes the smallest things take up the most room in your heart." –Winnie the Pooh

469 "He who can take advice is sometimes superior to him who can give it." – Erica Jong

470 "Sometimes it is more important to discover what one cannot do than what one can do." – Lin Yutang

471 "There's no such thing as quitting. Just sometimes there's a longer pause between relapses." – Alan Moore

472 "Sometimes the biggest problem is in your head. You've got to believe." – Jack Nicklaus

473 "Sometimes we stare so long at a door that is closing that we see too late the one that is open." – Alexander Graham Bell

Chapter 32

Hour Quotes

474 "To me every hour of the day and night is an unspeakably perfect miracle." –Walt Whitman

475 "If you have an hour, will you not improve that hour, instead of idling it away?" – Lord Chesterfield

476 "You can discover more about a person in an hour of play than in a year of conversation." – Plato

Chapter 33

Wisdom Quotes

477 "Our own physical body possesses a wisdom which we who inhabit the body lack. We give it orders which make no sense." – Henry Miller

478 "Turn your wounds into wisdom." – Oprah

479 "Wisdom is always an overmatch for strength." – Phil Jackson

480 "The beginning of wisdom is to call things by their right names." – Chinese Proverb

481 "Great doubts deep wisdom. Small doubts little wisdom." – Chinese Proverbs

482 "Wisdom begins in wonder." – Socrates

483 "The teacher who is indeed wise does not bid you to enter the house of his wisdom but,leads you to the threshold of your mind." – Khalil Gibran

Chapter 34

World Quotes

484 "Let everyone sweep in front of his own door and the whole world will be clean." – Johann Wolfgang Von Goethe

485 "Though we travel the world over to find the beautiful, we must carry it with us or we find it not." – Ralph Waldo Emerson

486 "Tell the world what you intend to do, but first show it." – Napoleon Hill

487 "The world has so many lessons to teach you." – Oprah

488 "The first step before anyone else in the world believes it is that you have to believe it." – Will Smith

489 "Never bend your head. Always hold it high. Look the world straight in the eye." – Helen Keller

490 "I consider this world to be like a school and our lives to be the classrooms." – Oprah

491 "How wonderful is it that nobody need wait a single moment before starting to improve the world." – Anne Frank

492 "Don't cheat the world of your contribution. Give it what you've got." – Steven Pressfield

493 "Although the world is full of suffering, it is also full of the overcoming of it." – Helen Keller

494 "There is only one pretty child in the world & every mother has it." – Chinese Proverb

495 "The more man meditates upon good thoughts, the better will be his world & the world at large." – Confucius

496 "Faith is the strength by which a shattered world shall emerge into the light." – Helen Keller

497 "The hand that rocks the cradle rules the world." – English proverbs

498 "The greatest way to live with honor in this world is to be what we pretend to be." – Socrates

499 "Laugh & the world laughs with you, weep & you weep alone." – English proverbs

500 "The world makes way for the man who knows where he is going." – Ralph Waldo Emerson

501 "A man sees in the world what he carries in his heart." – Johann Wolfgang Goethe

502 "My experience of the world is that things left to themselves don't get right." – T.H. Huxley

503 "A loving person lives in a loving world. A hostile person lives in a hostile world. Everyone you meet is your mirror." – Ken Keyes

504 "Do your little bit of good where you are; its those little bits of good put together that overwhelm the world." – Desmond Tutu

Chapter 35

Heart Quotes

505 "Have a heart that never hardens, and a temper that never tires, and a touch that never hurts." – Charles Dickens

506 "Create from the heart. Proceed with intelligence." – Danielle LaPorte

507 "Beauty is not in the face; beauty is a light in the heart." – Khalil Gibran

508 "If you look deep enough you will see music; the heart of nature being everywhere music." – Thomas Carlyle

509 "Winning is about heart, not just legs. It's got to be in the right place." – Lance Armstrong

510 "Always keep an open mind & a compassionate heart." – Phil Jackson

511 "It is only with the heart that one can see rightly; what is essential is invisible to the eye." – Antoine de Saint–Exupery

512 "If I keep a green bough in my heart, the singing bird will come." – Chinese Proverbs

513 "Every heart sings a song, incomplete, until another heart whispers back." – Plato

514 "Keep a green tree in your heart & perhaps a singing bird will come." – Chinese Proverb

515 "When you are sorrowful look again in your heart, and you shall see that in truth,you are weeping for that which has been your delight." – Gibran

516 "The worst prison would be a closed heart." – Pope John Paul II

Chapter 36

Passion Quotes

517 "The greatest gift is a passion for reading." – Elizabeth Hardwick

518 "Forget about the fast lane. If you really want to fly, just harness your power to your passion." – Oprah

519 "Only passions, great passions, can elevate the soul to great things." – Denis Diderot

520 "People spend their lives in the service of their passions instead of employing their passions in the service of their lives." – Richard Steele

Chapter 37

Joy Quotes

521 "Joy is the feeling of grinning inside." – Melba Colgrove

522 "If you do not enjoy what you are doing, you will never be good at it." – Luke Parker

523 "It is not joy that makes us grateful. It is gratitude that makes us joyful." – David Rast

524 In the midst of great joy, do not promise anyone anything. In the midst of great anger, do not answer anyone's letter." – Chinese Proverbs

525 "A joy shared is a joy doubled." – Anonymous

526 "One joy scatters a hundred griefs."– Chinese Proverbs

527 "To get the full value of a joy, you must have somebody to divide it with." – Mark Twain

Chapter 38

Moment Quotes

528 "Doing the best at this moment puts you in the best place for the next moment." – Oprah

529 "If you are patient in one moment of anger, you will escape a hundred days of sorrow." – Chinese Proverbs

530 "Breathe. Let go. & remind yourself that this very moment is the only one you know you have for sure." – Oprah

531 "In every contest, there comes a moment that separates winning from losing. The true warrior understands and seizes that moment." – Pat Riley

532 "Whatever the present moment contains, accept it as if you had chosen it." – Eckhart Tolle

533 "There comes a moment when you have to stop revving up the car and shove it into gear." – David Mahoney

Chapter 39

Achievement Quotes

534 "Never mistake activity for achievement." – John Wooden

535 "Optimism is the faith that leads to achievement. Nothing can be done without hope or confidence." – Helen Keller

536 "Make the most of yourself by fanning the tiny, inner sparks of possibility into flames of achievement." – Golda Meir

Part 2
Remarkable Quotes

Chapter 40

Selected Quotes

537 "Be what you are. This is the first step toward becoming better that you are." – Julius Charles Hare

538 "Always be a first–rate version of yourself, instead of a second–rate version of somebody else." – Judy Garland

539 "All mankind's inner feelings eventually manifest themselves as an outer reality." – Stuart Wilde

540 "You are the only person on earth who can use your ability." – Zig Ziglar

541 "I've decided that the stuff falling through the cracks is confetti and I'm having a party!" – Betsy Cañas Garmon

542 "Goodness is the only investment that never fails." –Henry David Thoreau

543 "Regardless of who you are or what you have been, you can be what you want to be." – W. Clement Stone

544 "If you are really thankful, what do you do? You share." – W. Clement Stone

545 "A man's worth is no greater than the worth of his ambitions." – Marcus Aurelius Antoninus

546 "All glory comes from daring to begin." – William Shakespeare

547 "The cave you fear to enter holds the treasure you seek." – Joseph Campbell

548 "Failure is not about insecurity. It's about lack of execution." – Jeffrey Gitomer

549 "For every good reason there is to lie, there is a better reason to tell the truth." – Bo Bennett

550 "If you don't have a competitive advantage, don't compete." – Jack Welch

551 "There was never a person who did anything worth doing that he did not receive more than he gave." – Henry Ward Beecher

552 "Hold yourself responsible for a higher standard than anybody expects of you. Never excuse yourself." – Henry Ward Beecher

553 "Winning isn't everything, but wanting to win is." – Vince Lombardi

554 "Surround yourself internally with the conditions you want to produce." – Wayne Dyer

555 "If everything seems under control, you're just not going fast enough." – Mario Andretti

556 "Don't just read the easy stuff. You may be entertained by it, but you will never grow from it." – Jim Rohn

557 "Be kind and merciful. Let no one ever come to you without coming away better and happier." – Mother Teresa

558 "If you listen to your fears, you will die never knowing what a great person you might have been." – Robert Schuller

559 "An optimist sees an opportunity in every calamity; a pessimist sees a calamity in every opportunity." –Winston Churchill

560 "Giving is better than receiving because giving starts the receiving process." – Jim Rohn

561 "Entrepreneurship is neither a science nor an art. It is a practice." – Peter Drucker

562 "Big pay and little responsibility are circumstances seldom found together." – Napoleon Hill

563 "Formal education will make you a living; self–education will make you a fortune." – Jim Rohn

564 "We cannot hold a torch to light another's path without brightening our own." – Ben Sweetland

565 "Face reality as it is, not as it was or as you wish it to be." – Jack Welch

566 "One person with a belief is equal to 99 who have only interests." – John Stuart Mill

567 "Make your product easier to buy than your competition, or you will find your customers buying from them, not you." – Mark Cuban

568 "To live in communion, in genuine dialogue with others is absolutely necessary if man is to remain human." – Thomas Merton

569 "Determine that the thing can and shall be done, and then we shall find the way." –Abraham Lincoln

570 "Belief consists in accepting the affirmations of the soul; unbelief, in denying them." – Ralph Waldo Emerson

571 "A handfull of patience is worth a bushel of brains." – Dutch Proverb

572 "If you want to test your memory, try to recall what you were worrying about one year ago today." – E. Joseph Cossman

573 "Gratitude is not only the greatest of virtues, but the parent of all others." – Cicero

574 "The more you explain it, the more I don't understand it." – Mark Twain

575 "Under certain circumstances, urgent circumstances, desperate circumstances, profanity provides a relief denied even to prayer." – Mark Twain

576 "My swearing doesn't mean any more to me than your sermons do to you." – Mark Twain

577 "Anger is an acid that can do more harm to the vessel in which it is stored than to anything on which it is poured." – Mark Twain

578 "To live in communion, in genuine dialogue with others is absolutely necessary if man is to remain human." – Thomas Merton

579 "We are tiny patches of the universe looking at itself and building itself." – John Wheeler

580 "If you haven't found something strange during the day, it hasn't been much of a day." – John Wheeler

581 "'I' is simply a phantom–like notion that arises & sets in the open, empty, ever–present awareness that you truly are." – John Wheeler

582 "The more you know the less you need to say." –Jim Rohn

583 "People who are unable to motivate themselves must be content with mediocrity, no matter how impressive their other talents." – Andrew Carnegie

584 "A library outranks any other one thing a community can do to benefit its people. It is a never failing spring in the desert." – Andrew Carnegie

585 "Today is the best preparation for what tomorrow may bring." – Andrew Carnegie

586 "It's easy to make a buck. It's a lot tougher to make a difference." – Tom Brokaw

587 "The most important question to ask is not what am I getting? The most important question to ask is What am I becoming?" – Jim Rohn

588 "Don't wish it were easier, wish you were better." – Jim Rohn

589 "Do not go where the path may lead; go instead where there is no path and leave a trail." – Ralph Waldo Emerson

590 "Always bear in mind that your own resolution to succeed is more important than any other." – Abraham Lincoln

591 "Foolish consistency is the hobgoblin of small minds." – Ralph Waldo Emerson

592 "Where the willingness is great, the difficulties cannot be great." – Niccolo Machiavelli

593 "You give but little when you give of your possessions. It is when you give of yourself that you truly give." – Khalil Gibran

594 "If you can't feed a hundred people, then just feed one." – Mother Teresa

595 "When you never listen to people, you're stubborn. When you always listen to people, you're not assertive." – Wilson Kanadi

596 "Let him who would be moved to convince others, be first moved to convince himself." – Thomas Carlyle

597 "If you don't know where you are going,you'll end up someplace else." – Yogi Berra

598 "Keep your eyes on the stars, and your feet on the ground." – Theodore Roosevelt

599 "Gardening is how I relax. It's another form of creating and playing with colors." – Oscar de la Renta

600 "In giving rights to others which belong to them, we give rights to ourselves and to our country." – John F. Kennedy

601 "If u reject the food, ignore the customs, fear the religion & avoid the people, u might better stay at home." – James Michener

602 "Perseverance allows you to get back on track when you hit a detour." – Catherine Pulsifer

603 "Be verbal in acknowledging your appreciation." – Catherine Pulsifer

604 "A mathematician is a device for turning coffee into theorems." – Paul Erdos

605 "Creativity is allowing yourself to make mistakes. Art is knowing which ones to keep." – Scott Adams

606 "Perseverance is not a long race; it is many short races one after another." – Walter Elliott

607 "The average estimate themselves by what they do, the above average by what they are." – Johann Friedrich Von Schiller

608 "When the wine goes in, strange things come out." – Johann Christoph Friedrich von Schiller

609 "What the inner voice says will not disappoint the hoping soul." – Friedrich von Schiller

610 "It is not only what we do, but what we do not do, for which we are accountable." – Moliere

611 "Always & never are two words you should always remember never to use." –Wendell Johnson

612 "Entrepreneurship is balancing unbridled optimism with intense skepticism." –Dan Eisenberg

613 "I'm not weird, I'm a limited edition." – Unknown

614 "If you do not conquer self, you will be conquered by self." – Napoleon Hill

615 "Remember sadness is always temporary. This, too, shall pass." – Chuck T. Falcon

616 "If the doors of perception were cleansed everything would appear to man as it is, infinite." – William Blake

617 "Those who restrain desire, do so because theirs is weak enough to be restrained." – William Blake

618 "He who desires, but acts not, breeds pestilence." – William Blake

619 "Faith is the confidence, the assurance, the enforcing truth, the knowing." – Robert Collier

620 "The mere fact that you have obstacles to overcome is in your favor..." – Robert Collier

621 "Men do less than they ought,unless they do all they can." – Thomas Carlyle

622 "Self is the only prison that can ever bind the soul." – Henry Van Dyke

623 "Knowing is not enough; we must apply.Willing is not enough; we must do." – Johann Wolfgang von Goethe

624 "A man who does not know foreign language is ignorant of his own." – Johann Wolfgang von Goethe

625 "Making good decisions is a crucial skill at every level." – Peter Drucker

626 "I always tried to turn every disaster into an opportunity." – John D. Rockefeller

627 "A man's errors are his portals of discovery." – James Joyce

628 "Experience is a hard teacher because she gives the test first, the lesson afterwards." – Vernon Law

629 "Fears are nothing more than a state of mind." – Napoleon Hill

630 "More gold has been mined from the thoughts of men than has been taken from the earth." – Napoleon Hill

631 "People tend to forget their duties but remember their rights." – Indira Ghandi

632 "We just need to keep this thing rolling. Get back in the race, keep winning ballgames." – Andy Green

633 "The important thing is not to stop questioning." –Albert Einstein

634 "Gluttony is an emotional sign that something is eating us." – Peter Devries

635 "A person of intellect without energy added to it, is a failure." – Sebastien–Roch Nicolas De Chamfort

636 "Reality is merely an illusion, albeit a very persistent one." – Albert Einstein

637 "Setting an example is not the main means of influencing another, it is the only means." – Albert Einstein

638 "Do not let what you cannot do interfere with what you can do." – John Wooden

639 "A coach is someone who gives correction without causing resentment." – John Wooden

640 "If you're not making mistakes, then you're not doing anything. I'm positive that a doer makes mistakes." – John Wooden

641 "Do right. Do your best. Treat others as you want to be treated." – Lou Holtz

642 "When I have fully decided that a result is worth getting I go ahead of it and make trial after until it comes." – Thomas Edison

643 "Few things help an individual more than to place responsibility upon him, and to let him know that You trust him." – Booker T. Washington

644 "Just because something doesn't do what you planned it to do doesn't mean it's useless." – Thomas Edison

645 "We can let circumstances rule us, or we can take charge and rule our lives from within." – Earl Nightingale

646 "We tend to live up to our expectations." – Earl Nightingale

647 "Nobody can bring you peace but yourself." – Ralph Waldo Emerson

648 "There is no absolute truth, only truth as it applies to you." – Oma Desala

649 "The only gift is a portion of thyself." – Ralph Waldo Emerson

650 "The greatest remedy for anger is delay. – Seneca

651 "We do not inherit the earth from our ancestors, we borrow it from our children." – Native American Proverb

652 "It takes one to know one." – American Proverb

653 "Whatever we do to the web, we do to ourselves. All things are bound together. All things connect." – Chief Seattle

654 "The years teach much what the days never knew." – Ralph Waldo Emerson

655 "When you cannot get a compliment in any other way pay yourself one." – Mark Twain

656 "Victory is always possible for the person who refuses to stop fighting." –Napoleon Hill

657 "The brick walls aren't there to keep us out, the brick walls are there to give us a chance to show how badly we want something." – R Pausch

658 "You'll never get ahead of anyone as long as you try to get even with him." – Lou Holtz

659 "Excellence is the best deterrent to racism or sexism." –Oprah

660 "You got to be careful if you don't know where you're going, because you might not get there." – Yogi Berra

661 "What you really want is to be surrounded by people you trust & treasure & by people who cherish you. That's when you're really rich." – Oprah

662 "Be thankful for what u have; you'll end up having more. If u concentrate on what u don't have, u will never, ever have enough." – Oprah

663 "Lots of people want to ride with u in the limo, but what u want is someone who will take the bus with u when the limo breaks down." – Oprah

664 "It's lack of faith that makes people afraid of meeting challenges, & I believed in myself." – Muhammad Ali

665 "I've always believed that everything is better when you share it." – Oprah

666 "You have to believe in yourself when no one else does– that makes you a winner right there." – Venus Williams

667 "If your mind is empty, it is always ready for anything." –Shunryu Suzuki

668 "I have a tip that can take 5 strokes off anyone's golf game. It's called an eraser." – Arnold Palmer

669 "It's important to give it all you have while you have the chance." – Shania Twain

670 "Once you make a decision, the universe conspires to make it happen." – R.W.E.

671 "Surround yourself with only people who are going to lift you higher." – Oprah

672 "Those who stand for nothing fall for anything." – Alexander Hamilton

673 "You can have it all. You just can't have it all at once." – Oprah

674 "A journey of a thousand miles must begin with a single step." – Lao Tsu

675 "Biology is the least of what makes someone a mother." – Oprah

676 "If you come to fame not understanding who you are, it will define who you are." – Oprah

677 "I had rather attempt something great & fail, than to attempt nothing at all & succeed." – Robert H. Schuller

678 "You are today where your thoughts have brought you. You will be tomorrow where your thoughts take you." – James Allen

679 "They who have conquered doubt and fear have conquered failure." – James Allen

680 "When you can't remember why you're hurt, that's when you're healed." – Jane Fonda

681 "It does not matter how slowly you go so long as you do not stop." – Confucius

682 "If you do what you've always done, you'll get what you've always gotten." – Tony Robbins

683 "What lies behind us & what lies before us are tiny matters compared to what lies within us." – Ralph Waldo Emerson

684 "Activity is contagious." – Ralph Waldo Emerson

685 "There is a lesson in almost everything that you do, and getting the lesson is how you move forward. It is how you enrich your spirit." – Oprah

686 "When you are kind 2 someone in trouble, u hope they'll remember & be kind to someone else, & it'll become like a wildfire." – Whoopi Goldberg

687 "That is really why we are here, to evolve as human beings. To grow into being more of ourselves." – Oprah

688 "We are called human beings not human doings. It's who you are not what you do that matters." – Rick Warren

689 "Conflict cannot survive without your participation." – Wayne Dyer

690 "How could you reach the pearl by only looking at the sea? If you seek the pearl, be a diver." – Rumi

691 "Take the first step in faith. You don't have to see the whole staircase, just take the first step. – Martin Luther King Jr.

692 "Sure the fight was fixed. I fixed it with a right hand." – George Foreman

693 "You can stand tall without standing on someone. You can be a victor without having victims." – Harriet Woods,

694 "Team guts always beat individual greatness." – Bob Zuppke

695 "Give advice; if people don't listen, let adversity teach them." – Ethiopian Proverb

696 "When spiders webs come together they can tie down a lion." – Ethiopian Proverb

697 "You can't catch a cub without going into the tiger's den." – Chinese Proverb

698 "Habits are cobwebs at first; cables at last." – Chinese Proverbs

699 "My choice; my responsibility; win or lose, only I hold the keys to my destiny." – Elain Maxwell

700 "Where there is no struggle, there is no strength." – Oprah

701 "Every artist dips his brush in his own soul, & paints his own nature into his pictures." – Henry Ward Beecher

702 "I still have my feet on the ground, I just wear better shoes." – Oprah

703 "If you're in pain, help someone else's pain, & when you're in a mess, u get yourself out of the mess helping someone out of theirs." – Oprah

704 "Fear can keep us up all night long, but faith makes one fine pillow." – Unknown

705 "If a man wants you, nothing can keep him away. If he doesn't, nothing can make him stay." – Oprah

706 "For a man to conquer himself is the first & noblest of all victories." – Plato

707 "Difficulties in live are intended to make us better, not bitter." – Dan Reeves

708 "Getting people to like you is merely the other side of liking them." – Norman Peale

709 "It always seems impossible until its done." – Nelson Mandela

710 "It is hard to fail, but it is worse never have tried to succeed." – Theodore Roosevelt

711 "It is thought & feeling which guides the universe, not deeds." – Edgar Cayce

712 "People will forget what U said, people will forget what U did, but people will never forget how U made them feel." – Maya Angelou

713 "I believe the most important single thing, beyond discipline & creativity is daring to dare." – Maya Angelou

714 "To everyone is given the key to heaven; the same key opens the gates of hell." – Ancient Proverb

715 "Not everybody can be famous. But everybody can be great, because greatness is determined by service." – Martin Luther King

716 "Forgive yourself for your faults & your mistakes & move on." – Les Brown

717 "Peace cannot be kept by forced. It can only be achieved by understanding." – Albert Einstein

718 "Worry often gives a small thing a great shadow." – Swedish Proverb

719 "Before you can win, you have to believe you are worthy." – Mike Ditka

720 "If you are not generous with a meager income, you will never be generous with abundance." – Harold Nye

721 "A man needs a little madness or else he never dares to cut the rope & be free." – Nikos Kazantazkis

722 "Only that which is temporary endures." – French proverb

723 "Do the hard jobs first. The easy jobs will take care of themselves." – Dale Carnegie

724 "It's hard to beat a person who never gives up." – Babe Ruth

725 "The expression a woman wears on her face is far more important than the clothes she wears on her back." – Dale Carnegie

726 "Don't cry because its over. Smile because it happened." – Dr. Seuss

727 "The less you know, the more you believe." – Bono

728 "Adversity causes some men to break; others to break records." – William Arthur Ward

729 "Ignorance of one's misfortunes is clear gain." – Greek Proverb

730 "It is our light, not our darkness that most frightens us." – Marianne Williamson

731 "Take responsibility for yourself.., because no one's going to take responsibility for you." – Tyra Banks

732 "I am the greatest, I said that even before I knew I was". – Muhammad Ali

733 "Always give without remembering & always receive without forgetting". – Brian Tracy

734 "Our deepest fear is not that we are inadequate. Our deepest fear is that we are powerful beyond measure." – Marianne Williamson

735 "Your mistake does not define who you are...you are your possibilities." – Oprah

736 "Better to remain silent & be thought a fool that to speak & remove all doubt." – English proverbs

737 "As for me, all I know is that I know nothing." – Socrates

738 "If it wasn't hard, everyone would do it. It's the hard that makes it great." – Tom Hanks

739 "The ones who want to achieve & win championships motivate themselves." – Mike Ditka

740 "A bird in your hand is worth more than 100 in the forest." – Chinese Proverbs

741 "You're never a loser until you quit trying." – Mike Ditka

742 "When anyone tells me I can't do anything...I'm just not listening anymore." – Florence Griffith–Joyner

743 "Worrying never did anyone any good." – English proverbs

745 "You can easily judge the character of a man by how he treats those who can do nothing for him." – James D. Miles

746 "One who is injured ought not to return the injury, for on no account can it be right to do an injustice." – Socrates

747 "I am an optimist. It does not seem too much use being anything else." – Winston Churchill

748 "A book is like a garden carried in the pocket." – Chinese Proverb

749 "Strength does not come from winning. Your struggles develop your strengths." – Arnold Schwarzenegger

750 "Age is no guarantee of maturity." – Lawana Blackwell

751 "In a crisis, don't hide behind anything or anybody. They are going to find you anyway." – Bear Bryant

752 "The earth provides enough to satisfy ever man's needs, but not every man's greed." – Gandhi

753 "Once a word leaves your mouth, you cannot chase it back even with the swiftest horse." – Chinese Proverbs

754 "He who sacrifices his conscience to ambition burns a picture to obtain the ashes." – Chinese Proverbs

755 "No one has ever made himself great by showing how small someone else is." – Irvin Himmel

756 "The more I practice, the luckier I get." – Jerry Barber

757 "Others can stop you temporarily – you are the only one who can do it permanently." – Zig Ziglar

758 "All a girl really wants is for one guy to prove to her that they are not all the same." – Marilyn Monroe

759 "Teachers open the door but you must walk through it yourself." – Chinese Proverbs

760 "It is never too late to be what you might have been." – George Eliot

761 "Lessons often come dressed up as detours and roadblocks." – Oprah

762 "Be a good listener. Your ears will never get you in trouble." – Frank Tyger

763 "Minds are like parachutes – they only function when open." – Thomas Dewar

764 "Great spirits have always faced violent opposition from mediocre minds." – Einstein

765 "You can't live a perfect day without doing something for someone who will never be able to repay you." – John Wooden

766 "Most people never run far enough on their first wind to find out they've got a second." – William James

767 "A man who correctly guesses a woman's age may be smart, but he's not very bright." – Lucille Ball

768 "There's none so blind as those who will not see." – English proverbs

769 "You cannot escape the responsibility of tomorrow by evading it today." – Abraham Lincoln

770 "A woman is like a tea bag: you cannot tell how strong she is until you put her in hot water." – Nancy Reagan

771 "Baseball is ninety percent mental & the other half is physical." – Yogi Berra

772 "I was wise enough to never grow up while fooling most people into believing I had." – Margaret Mead

773 "It is easy to dodge a spear that comes in front of you but hard to keep harms away from an arrow shot from behind." – Chinese Proverbs

774 "Talent wins games, but teamwork & intelligence win championships." – Michael Jordan

775 "Perfection is not attainable, but if we chase perfection we can catch excellence." – Vince Lombardi

776 "Freedom consists not in doing what we like, but in having the right to do what we ought." – Pope John Paul II

777 "Advice is what we ask for when we already know the answer but wish we didn't." – Erica Jong

778 "It is the mark of an educated mind to be able to entertain a thought without accepting it." – Aristotle

779 "Laws control the lesser man. Right conduct controls the greater one." – Chinese proverb

780 "When things r against u, remember airplanes takes off against the wind, not with it." – Henry Ford

781 "Accept challenges so that you may feel the exhilaration of victory." – Unknown

782 "Each person you meet is Jesus in disguise." – Mother Teresa

783 "Ninety–nine percent of the failures comes from people who have the habit of making excuses." – George W. Carve

784 "Every day do something that will inch you closer to a better tomorrow." – Doug Firebaugh

785 "However long the night, the dawn will break." – African Proverb

786 "We all must try 2 be th best person we can: by making th best choices, by making th most of th talents we've been given." – Mary Lou Retton

787 "Only when we are no longer afraid do we begin to live." – Dorothy Thompson

788 "Excellence is not a singular act but a habit. You are what you do repeatedly." – Shaquille O'Neal

789 "A hundred men may make an encampment, but it takes a woman to make a home." – Chinese Proverbs

790 "Things turn out best for the people who make the best of the way things turn out." – John Wooden

791 "It isn't enough to talk about peace. One must believe in it. & it isn't enough to believe in it. One must work at it." – Eleanor Roosevelt

792 "The word liberal comes from the word free. We must cherish and honor the word free or it will cease to apply to us." – Eleanor Roosevelt

793 "You were born to win, but to be a winner, you must plan to win, prepare to win, & expect to win." – Zig Ziglar

794 "There are 3 types of baseball players: those who make it happen, those who watch it happen, & those who wonder what happens." – Tommy Lasorda

795 "Remember always that you not only have the right to be an individual, you have an obligation to be one." – Eleanor Roosevelt

796 "If you don't risk anything, you risk even more." – Erica Jong

797 "Do what you can, with what you have, where you are." – Theodore Roosevelt

798 "A single conversation across the table with a wise man is worth a month's study of books." – Chinese Proverbs

799 "The smallest deed is better than the greatest intention." – John Burroughs

800 "The worst thing about being lied to is simply knowing you weren't worth the truth." – Unknown

801 "When one's expectations are reduced to zero, one really appreciates everything one does have." – Stephen Hawking

802 "Education is the best provision for old age." – Aristotle

803 "He that takes medicine and neglects diet, wastes the skill of the physician." – Chinese Proverb

804 "You can't let praise or criticism get to you. It's a weakness to get caught up in either one." – John Wooden

805 "Decide that you want it more than you are afraid of it." – Bill Cosby

806 "Danger 4 most of us lies not in setting our aim too high & falling short; but in setting our aim 2 low & achieving our mark." – Michaelangelo

807 "The way I see it, if you want the rainbow, you gotta put up with the rain." – Dolly Parton

808 "One man practicing sportsmanship is far better than a hundred teaching it." – Knute Rockne

809 "The difference between the impossible and the possible lies in a man's determination." – Tommy Lasorda

810 "Never let your head hang down. Never give up and sit down and grieve. Find another way." – Satchel Paige

811 "Alone we can do so little; together we can do so much." – Helen Keller

812 "We do not quit playing because we grow old, we grow old because we quit playing." – Oliver Wendell Holmes

813 "I never did anything worth doing by accident." – Plato

814 "Smooth seas do not make skillful sailors." – African proverb

815 "You can't turn back the clock. But you can wind it up again." – Bonnie Prudden

816 "The game is my wife. It demands loyalty & responsibility, & it gives me back fulfillment & peace." – Michael Jordan

817 "Cherish forever what makes you unique, 'cuz you're really a yawn if it goes." – Bette Midler

818 "When you reread a classic you do not see more in the book than you did before; you see more in you than was there before." – Clifton Fadiman

819 "People only do their best at things they truly enjoy." – Jack Nicklaus

820 "The difference in winning & losing is most often, not quitting." – Walt Disney

821 "You can out–distance that which is running after you, but not what is running inside you." – Rwandan proverb

822 "You cannot help men permanently by doing for them what they could & should do for themselves." – Abraham Lincoln

823 "Face your deficiencies and acknowledge them. But do not let them master you." – Hellen Keller

824 "The purpose of our lives is to give birth to the best which is within us." – Marianne Williamson

825 "What is told into the ear of a man is often heard a hundred miles away." – Chinese Proverbs

826 "I always prefer to believe in the best of everybody – it saves so much trouble." – Rudyard Kipling

827 "I can accept failure. Everyone fails at something. But I can't accept not trying." – Michael Jordan

828 "A gem cannot be polished without friction, nor a man perfected without trials." – Chinese Proverbs

829 "Resolve never to quit, never to give up, no matter what the situation." – Jack Nicklaus

830 "From the deepest desires often come the deadliest hate." – Socrates

831 "The trouble with most of us is that we would rather be ruined by praise than saved by criticism." – Norman Peale

832 "The men who try to do something & fail are infinitely better than those who try to do nothing & succeed." – L.Jones

833 "Be faithful in small things because it is in them that your strength lies." – Mother Teresa

834 "Difficulties in live are intended to make us better, not bitter." – Dan Reeves

835 "It's never crowded along the extra mile." – Dr. Wayne Dyer

836 "Early to bed & early to rise, makes a man healthy, wealthy & wise." – English proverbs

837 "When you believe in a thing, believe in it all the way, implicitly & unquestionably." – Walt Disney

838 "I have become my own version of an optimist... Something terrific will come no matter how dark the present." – Joan Rivers

839 "The only way to maximize potential for performance is to be calm in the mind." – Brian Sipe

840 "I count him braver who overcomes his desires than him who conquers his enemies; for the hardest victory is over self." – Aristotle

841 "Wherever you go, no matter what the weather, always bring your own sunshine." – Anthony J. D'Angelo

842 "We are what we repeatedly do. Excellence, then, is not an act, but a habit." – Aristotle

843 "Dignity does not consist in possessing honors, but in deserving them." – Aristotle

844 "When you can't remember why you're hurt, that's when you're healed." – Jane Fonda

845 "Experience is a comb which nature gives to men when they are bald." – Chinese Proverbs

846 "Being powerful is like being a lady. If you have to tell people you are, you aren't." – Margaret Thatcher

847 "The rich would have to eat money if the poor did not provide food." – Russian Proverb

848 "We cannot become what we need to be by remaining what we are." – Max De Pree

849 "Old age is like a plane flying through a storm. Once you're aboard, there's nothing you can do." – Golda Meir

850 "If you want something done, ask a busy person to do it. The more things you do, the more you can do." – Lucille Ball

851 "It's not the load that breaks you down, it's the way you carry it." – Lou Holtz

852 "Act as if what you do makes a difference. It does." – William James

853 "I shut my eyes in order to see." – Paul Gauguin

854 "Being able to touch so many people through my businesses and make money while doing it, is a huge blessing." – Magic Johnson

855 "If you do build a great experience, customers tell each other about that. Word of mouth is very powerful." – Jeff Bezos

856 "The few who do are the envy of the many who only watch." – Jim Rohn

857 "Always seek out the seed of triumph in every adversity." – Og Mandino

858 "You can do anything you wish to do, have anything you wish to have, be anything you wish to be." – Robert Collier

859 "Nothing can bring you peace but yourself ." – Ralph Waldo Emerson

860 "The grass must bend when the wind blows across it." – Confucius

861 "If a man is proud of his wealth, he should not be praised until it is known how he employs it." – Socrates

862 "The older the fiddler, the sweeter the tune." – English Proverb

863 "Once you pour the water out of the bucket it's hard to get it back in it." – Chinese Proverbs

864 "We do not act rightly because we have virtue or excellence, but we rather have those because we have acted rightly." – Aristotle

865 "Youth is wasted on the young." – English proverbs

866 "One never needs their humor as much a when they argue with a fool." – Chinese Proverbs

867 "It is not living that matters, but living rightly." – Socrates

868 "Talk doesn't cook rice." – Chinese Proverbs

869 "Do what you know is right & importance, it is the highroad to pride, self–esteem, & personal satisfaction." – Margaret Thatcher

870 "Suffering becomes beautiful when 1 bears great calamities w/ cheerfulness,not through insensibility but through greatness of mind." – Aristotle

871 "Better a little which is well done, than a great deal imperfectly." – Plato

872 "Every path has its puddle." – English proverb

873 "The great question is not whether you have failed, but whether you are content with failure." – Chinese Proverb

874 "Giving your son a skill is better than giving him one thousand pieces of gold." – Chinese Proverb

875 "Habits are first cobwebs, then cables." – Spanish Proverb

876 "A man grows most tired while standing still." – Chinese Proverbs

877 "You cannot prevent the birds of sorrow from flying over your head, but u can prevent them from building nests in your hair." – Chinese Proverbs

878 "What would you attempt to do if you knew you could not fail?" – Unknown

879 "Better a diamond with a flaw than a pebble without one." – Chinese Proverbs

880 "To be uncertain is to be uncomfortable, but to be certain is to be ridiculous." – Chinese Proverbs

881 "If you win through bad sportsmanship, that's no real victory." – Babe Zaharias

882 "I ask not for a lighter burden, but for broader shoulders." – Jewish proverb

883 "A book holds a house of gold." – Chinese Proverbs

884 "Sow much, reap much; sow little, reap little." – Chinese Proverbs

885 "It is better to look ahead & prepare than to look back & regret." – Jackie Joyner–Kersee

886 "Climb mountains to see lowlands." – Chinese Proverbs

887 "If your strength is small, don't carry heavy burdens. If your words are worthless, don't give advice." – Chinese Proverbs

888 "Flowing water never goes bad; our door hubs never gather termites." – Chinese Proverbs

889 "The greatest virtues are those which are most useful to other persons." – Aristotle

890 "Idleness is the mother of all vices." – Russian proverb

891 "Nature does nothing in vain." – Aristotle

892 "The tongue can paint what the eye can't see." – Chinese Proverbs

893 "The roots of education are bitter, but the fruit is sweet." – Aristotle

894 "A fall into a ditch makes you wiser." – Chinese Proverbs

895 "A great fortune depends on luck, a small one on diligence." – Chinese Proverbs

896 "Those that know, do. Those that understand, teach." – Aristotle

897 "Quality is not an act, it is a habit." – Aristotle

898 "There are two things a person should never be angry at, what they can help, & what they cannot." – Plato

899 "For remember, fear doesn't exist anywhere except in the mind." – Dale Carnegie

900 "Different flowers look good to different people." – Chinese Proverbs

901 "By nature, men are nearly alike; by practice, they get to be wide apart." – Confucius

902 "Beauty is a short–lived tyranny." – Socrates

903 "The aim of art is to represent not the outward appearance of things, but their inward significance." – Aristotle

904 "At his best, man is the noblest of all animals; separated from law & justice he is the worst." – Aristotle

905 "Everything has its beauty but not everyone sees it." – Confucius

906 "Excellence is an art won by training & habituation." – Aristotle

907 "You'll never plow a field by turning it over in your mind." – Irish proverb

908 "The saving man becomes the free man." – Chinese Proverbs

909 "There is no pillow so soft as a clear conscience." – French proverb

910 "Promises are like crying babies in a theater, they should be carried out at once." – Norman Peale

911 "When a father gives to his son, both laugh; when a son gives to his father, both cry." – Jewish Proverb

912 "The drowning man is not troubled by rain."
– Persian Proverb

913 "The more you sweat in practice, the less you bleed in battle." – Unknown

914 "Live for today for tomorrow never comes."
– English proverbs

915 "He who asks the question is a fool for a minute; he who does not is a fool forever." – Chinese Proverbs

916 "All paid jobs absorb & degrade the mind." – Aristotle

917 "Youth is easily deceived because it is quick to hope." – Aristotle

918 "Worthless people live only to eat & drink; people of worth eat & drink only to live." – Socrates

919 "If you do not study hard when young you'll end up bewailing your failures as you grow up." – Chinese Proverbs

920 "What it lies in our power to do, it lies in our power not to do." – Aristotle

921 "If you wish to know the mind of a man, listen to his words." – Chinese Proverbs

922 "Once the game is over, the king & the pawn go back in the same box."   Italian Proverb

923 "Good habits formed at youth make all the difference." – Aristotle

924 "The greatest conqueror is he who overcomes the enemy without a blow." – Chinese Proverbs

925 "Do not call to a dog with a whip in your hand." – Zululand Proverb

926 "Insanity is doing the same thing in the same way & expecting a different outcome." – Chinese Proverbs

927 "Enough shovels of earth – a mountain. Enough pails of water – a river." – Chinese Proverbs

928 "No great genius has ever existed without some touch of madness." – Aristotle

929 "Respect yourself & others will respect you." – Confucius

930 "You can't tell a book by looking at its cover." – English proverbs

931 "Never do anything standing that you can do sitting, or anything sitting that you can do lying down." – Chinese Proverb

932 "He who is to be a good ruler must have first been ruled." – Aristotle

933 "A Jade stone is useless before it is processed; a man is good–for–nothing until he is educated." – Chinese Proverbs

934 "A people that values its priviliges over its principles soon loses both." – Dwight Eisenhower

935 "The more informative your advertising, the more persuasive it will be." – David Ogilvy

936 "To climb steep hills requires a slow pace at first." – Shakespeare

937 "If you don't fail now and again, it's a sign you're playing it safe." – Woody Allen

938 "Once you replace negative thoughts with positive ones, you'll start having positive results." – Willie Nelson

939 "Giving up is the ultimate tragedy." – Robert Donovan

940 "Kind words can be short and easy to speak, but their echoes are truly endless." – Mother Teresa

941 "Everything that irritates us about others can lead us to an understanding of ourselves." – Carl Jung

942 "There's no limit to what a man can achieve, if he doesn't care who gets the credit." – Laing Burns, Jr.

943 "There are a thousand excuses for every failure but never a good reason." – Mark Twain

944 "I quit being afraid when my first venture failed and the sky didn't fall down." – Allen H. Neuharth

945 "Ninety–nine percent of failures come from people who have the habit of making excuses." – George Washington Carver

946 "There is no such thing as natural touch. Touch is something you create by hitting millions of golf balls." – Lee Trevino

947 "We are made to persist. That's how we find out who we are." – Tobias Wolff

948 "The thing always happens that you really believe in; and the belief in a thing makes it happen." – Frank Lloyd Wright

949 "Who has not served cannot command." – John Florio

950 "The man who is swimming against the stream knows the strength of it." – Woodrow Wilson

951 "Make yourself necessary to somebody." – Ralph Waldo Emerson

952 "A bold, vigorous assault has won many a faltering cause." – Ira Eaker

953 "Hanging onto resentment is letting someone you despise live rent–free in your head." – Esther Lederer

954 "People will forget what you said, people will forget what you did, but people will never forget how you made them feel." – Maya Angelou

955 "Accept the challenges so that you may feel the exhilaration of victory." – George Patton

956 "Praise is a powerful people–builder. Catch individuals doing something right." – Brian Tracy

957 "He that waits upon fortune is never sure of a dinner." – Benjamin Franklin

958 "I was taught that the way of progress is neither swift nor easy." – Marie Curie

959 "It isn't where you came from; it's where you're going that counts." – Ella Fitzgerald

960 "Every artist was first an amateur." – Ralph Waldo Emerson

961 "Nothing is easy to the unwilling." – Thomas Fuller

962 "Without faith, nothing is possible. With it, nothing is impossible." – Mary Bethune

963 "Your mind is the only thing you control exclusively. Don't give it away too freely through useless arguments." – Napoleon Hill

964 "Never attack a problem without also presenting a solution." – Jim Rohn

965 "We often take for granted the very things that most deserve our gratitude." – Cynthia Ozick

966 "Anyone who keeps the ability to see beauty never grows old." – Franz Kafka

967 "Inspire your teams and lead by example and your business will be ahead of the game." – Mike Spicer

968 "Just swimming was something I would never do . I would always set a task." – Michael Gross

969 "Too many people overvalue what they are not and undervalue what they are." – Malcolm Forbes

970 "I've felt that dissatisfaction is the basis of progress. When we become satisfied in business, we become obsolete." – J. Willard Marriott Sr

971 "Pay attention. Don't just stagger through the day." – Jim Rohn

972 "Always look at what you have left. Never look at what you have lost." – Robert Schuller

973 "Never look down on anybody unless you're helping him up." – Jesse Jackson

974 "Always tell the truth, then you dont have to remember anything." – Mark Twain

975 "If you dont read the newspaper you are uninformed. If you do read the newspaper you are misinformed." – Mark Twain

976 "You have to do more than you get paid for because that's where the fortune is." – Jim Rohn

977 "High expectations are the key to everything." – Sam Walton

978 "Purpose and laughter are the twins that must not separate. Each is empty without the other." – Robert K. Greenleaf

979 "You dont start living until u can rise above the narrow confines of Ur individualistic concerns to the broader concerns of all humanity." – MLK

980 "A man is rich in proportion to the number of things he can afford to let alone." – Henry David Thoreau

981 "True grit is making a decision and standing by it, doing what must be done." – John Wayne

982 "Failure should be our teacher, not our undertaker. Failure is delay not defeat. It is a temporary detour, not a dead end." – Denis Waitley

983 "Patience and perseverance have a magical effect before which difficulties disappear and obstacles vanish." – John Quincy Adams

984 "You can't talk yourself out of a problem you behave yourself into." – Stephen Covey

985 "Determine never to be idle. It is wonderful how much may be done if we are always doing." – Thomas Jefferson

986 "Your greatness is measured by your horizons." – Michelangelo

987 "Ninety percent of all those who fail are not actually defeated. They simply quit." – Paul J. Meyer

988 "It's not where you start – it's where you finish that counts." – Zig Ziglar

989 "Our minds can shape the way a thing will be because we act according to our expectations." – Federico Fellini

990 "The first great gift we can bestow on others is a good example." – Thomas Morell

"Don't let what you can't do stop you from doing what you can do." – John Wooden

991 "In the middle of every difficulty comes opportunity." – Albert Einstein

992 "You can't do it unless you can imagine it." – George Lucas

993 "All that is necessary to break the spell of inertia and frustration is this: Act as if it were impossible to fail." – Dorothea Brande

994 "Evidence is conclusive that your self–talk has a direct bearing on your performance." – Zig Ziglar

995 "Avoid having your ego so close to your position that when your position falls, your ego goes with it." – Colin Powell

996 "The only thing we have to fear is fear itself." – Franklin D. Roosevelt

997 "If somebody has to tell you how good he is every step of the way, he probably is not." – Zig Ziglar

998 "To have true friends and be loved by them, we must in turn feel love and sympathy for others." – Dalai Lama

999 "You must make a decision that you are going to move on. It wont happen automatically." – Joel Osteen

1000 "Three things in Human Life are important: The first is to be kind. The second is to be kind. The Third is to be kind." – Mother Teresa

1001 "If you spend time with young people, You too will remain young. – Pope John Paul II

INDEX

www.ingramcontent.com/pod-product-compliance
Lightning Source LLC
Chambersburg PA
CBHW070806280326
41934CB00012B/3080